WHAT THERE WAS (OR
WHAT THERE WASN'T)

DORA MORRIGAN

WHAT THERE WAS (OR WHAT THERE WASN'T)

Dalygood Media, LLC

WHAT THERE WAS

I've been stabbed in the heart
But the only blood that flows
Are the words on this page

My pain too great
To hold within
To reveal in truth

Let these pages bind my wound
Let these words stitch my scars
Let this ink replace life lost

TIME

_____

Can you feel the ticking clock
Deep within your bones
The sound of time
Chipping away at your soul

The universe is a river
Where the current catches the flow
Careful now love
So that we are not swept away

SING

Sing to me, my heart.
Bring me to my knees.
Summon the best of me
So you can see the worst of it
Here, in the dark,
My thoughts and you.
My only two companions.

Keep me company. Keep me warm.
Keep the light in this dark night.

Don't let me drown.

A SHORT PRAYER

Dear God

What the fuck

I trust in You, I have faith in You and Your plan

But please give me the strength to bear it

Because what the fuck

I intend to shine with or without you
But imagine how bright I'd be
With your light upon me

UPDATE FROM DAY 90 OF QUARANTINE

I say I'm not fine, but it's fine.
There are worse quarantines than mine.

To match my echoes day after day
To never have the loneliness ever go away.

The lies my memories whisper to me
Begging me to succumb to the fantasy

Oh fire, oh fire, let me be warm
Do not ever let this be my new norm

The final ripple of the stone cast
Hit my feet, an echo of the past

To truly laugh and smile
For it has been quite a while

I am not fine, but it is fine.
For there are worse quarantines than mine

I am forgotten in the face of misery
I have fallen through reality

To sleep, to walk, to eat, to work
Until my sanity goes fully berserk.

Oh my fire, my fire,
my one heart's one desire.

Do you continue to burn?
Or shall I never learn?

How can I return to sanity?
How can I return to me?

The answer is that I can not
What I have is all I've got

I'm not fine, I'm not fine, this is not fine
And there are worse quarantines than mine.

HALF HOPE, HALF AGONY

Half hope, half agony
I hope you enjoyed the fantasy

It was fun to be lost in you
until ruined by what we had to do

Reality awoken me
to our half hope, half agony

Every dream must end
And every wound must tend

To our half hope, half agony
Drowning in shared misery

SURRENDER TO THE CHAOS

———————————

Surrender to the chaos
Baptize in the new reality

You know me
You knew me

You've said good bye so long ago
It feels like we never did

Come over, I whisper to the stars
Come over, I whisper to the void
Come over, come over, come over

And join in this baptism with me.
Be the salvation I pray for you to be.

Do not let me drown.
Do not let me down.
Do not let my bare feet leave the ground

And float up and up and up
To a world not of yours

Feel my words whisper into your mind
As yours haunt mine

Do you not feel my light shine?
Do you not think of me in the rain?

There is chaos in my brain
But only you in my heart.

And I cannot tell which shall drown me first

GOLDEN POPPIES

————————————

Like the Golden Poppies, I grow best after a fire.
When something tries to push me down, I come up
higher.

Like a Sunflower, I always face the sun.
Never a day goes by without some fun.

Like a Tulip, I aspire for fame.
I simply want everybody to know how to spell my
name.

Like a Rose, I'm a hopeless romantic.
My heart is quite gigantic.

So like a Violet, I'm going to be humble.
And stop this poem before I fumble.

I'm crying tears that move without effort
I'm mourning a death that never died
I'm wallowing for a love that was never mine
I'm suffering for a soul that never loved

PORTRAIT OF A DEMISEXUAL

"Don't have sex. It's a sin." Teachers warn in middle
school.
"Okay no problem." I say.

"Don't have sex. You could get pregnant." Media
warns in high school.
"Okay no problem." I say.

"Don't have sex. You could get an STD." Nurses warn
in college.
"Okay no problem." I say.

"You're 26 and haven't had sex yet?" Friends ques-
tion after drinks.
"Oh, this is a problem." I think.

Cast me as the vixen in your witch hunt
Condemn me with your salvation
Bless me with your damnation
Tie me to the stake and let your justice fuel the
flames
But remember as you set me to burn
That you are just as innocent as I

How do I never feel love again?
The same way you strip the sunset of its color.

AN APOLOGY

I'm sorry I couldn't be the person I am today for you
yesterday
But I needed to experience yesterday to get to today.

I'm sorry you had to be a stepping stone and not the
final destination.
I'm sorry you had to see the worst of me so I could
find the best of myself.

I'm not sorry I changed.

AN ODE TO MY FIRST LOVE

You're the bile in the back of my throat.
We've been together all of my life and I can't stand
you.
You've hurt me.
Cursed me with madness.
Burned my skin and halted my breath.
Claimed me from my friends without the slightest
apology.
Forced me into your arms every weekend.
You destroy my friends.
You destroy families.
You're a monster in your own right.
With your selfish and corrupt ways.
My survival with you is a miracle.
You've brought me only pain and weakness.
Yet I can't stand the thought of a world without you.
You've given me strength.
Replenished my hope and fulfilled my dreams.
When I cannot smile, you give me a reason to.
With you, I'm invincible.
With you, I'm weak.
Addicted to your fulfilling ways.

Rare moments of triumph sustain my return to you.
I am nothing short of a desperate mistress.
But your love has grown old.
Yet I cannot bring myself to say no.
The world does not want us together.

And neither do I.

Yet I can't bring myself to say good-bye.

RELEASE ME

———————————

To feel your sweetness once again
would be the most blessed curse upon my life

I am the trouble but you are a danger
and I keep falling headfirst into the flames

I aspire for a life where the memory of you
does not condemn my shadows
I aspire for a life where the memory of you
fills the breath of my lungs

To aspire for you is my most unholy sin
To desire you feels like heaven in hell

I wish to hear my name from your lips
in screams, in whispers, in moments only for us

I wish to never hear of your name again
in screams, in whispers, in moments only for me

To love you has felt like a weight
To love you is my prayer to be free

Release me and my love
but only after I do so first.

SUMMER NIGHT

You are as beautiful as a summer night.
When the heat of midday cools to a simmer
And a soft breeze kisses my skin in your place.
Without the crisp chill of fall or the cool anticipation
of spring.
When orange and purple and pink dance in the sky
with vibrance.
The scent of smoking hickory and wood drifts
around us
The memories of the day warming me
But the anticipation for the night exciting me
For once the colors fade, joining the soft breeze,
We are welcomed by the stars as they sing for us
Telling the stories of our past and of to become
And we dance underneath them
Barefoot on the kind grass, brittle from the heat
But strengthened by the season
Enamored by the quiet
For the music quiets and the hum of summer takes
hold.
And I hold you, as beautiful as a summer night.
And I adore you just the same.

Do the storms only occur at night
because they know no one is awake to witness them

Or do they wish to rage without ruining the day

THE QUIET OF NOTHING

_____

As I wait for my food to cook
As your reply is delayed
As the snow falls softly, dashing before it can exist
As night ages and refines darkness
As nothing at all happens all at once

THE STORY OF US

What will the story of us say about you and I?
Does it start with the soft hello and end with the
tearful good-bye?

Or do we have a tale that never ends?
That twists and turns and rises and bends?

Where the chapters grow long
And our choices are never wrong?

Where do we fit on the shelf with our book?
Is horror or romance where people go to look?

With the way you look at me
I'd find us in spirituality.

Darling don't you know
It's easier to be heartless
Than it is to be unloved.

I'M DRUNK. TAKE ME HOME.

Let me tell you of my dream
And all it may seem

I go out for food
And you're in a mood

You want to think
But I want to drink

We laugh, we cry
Your presence is a high

Then it's the end
And we follow the wind

I'm drunk, take me home
And then we're alone.

You're always in my head
You're never in my heart.

We can change that tonight.
We can make things right.

I'm drunk. You take me home.
We're no longer alone.

UNDONE

————————————

I'm coming undone with you.
I am so lost within you.
I gave you everything about me.
The only truth you can't hold against me
is the one I hold deepest within me.
The one that will truly undo me if you ever discover it.
You can unravel me thread by thread.
But you will never know me until you know the love
I hold for you.
The kind of thing that will have me follow you to
the edge of the world
even if I have to be the one to step off the cliff.
You have all of me in the palm of your hand.
Just don't use it against me.
Please.
Have mercy as you hold me.

If you look at me like I'm the world
And I look at you like you're the universe itself
Then what a galaxy we make.

Can it happen twice
But why would you burn
Twice
When you can die
Once

DRUNK & LOVE

I'm a little drunk now,
which means I'm a lot sexy.

Could go for a kiss, could go for a fuck.
Could go for anything if I had any luck

Let me make you smile
Let you make me smile.

Let's make this last a while

Only if you were there.
Only if you were here.

Let me kiss you,
Let you kiss me.

I'm so in love
and you're so drunk.

I'm so drunk
and you're so in love.

Let me feel your warmth,
let you feel my cold.

Let our hearts become one
as the whiskey bottle becomes done.

This whiskey does a lot better of talking than me
You do a lot better of listening than me.

Even when we're odd,
You're oddly so even for me.

I'm so drunk,
I'm so in love,
And there's never been a worse combination with you.

WERE TO GO

If I were to go, would I be a bright light dim too soon?
Or a thank God and good riddance to that crazy loon

Perhaps more so I'd just be another soul long gone
Already forgotten before the dawn

How long would my memory claim your heart?
How long before I am lost for a fresh start?

Forget me not or forget me so
None of this I will ever know

For I will be gone and with the stars
Forgetting you as fast as the speeding cars

I dare you
to kneel before me
with such a hatred in your eyes
that you are forced to concede
that once upon a time
you felt for me
too

I LIKE ME

———————————

I like being strong.

> But sometimes I wish I weren't.
> So I can know comfort.

I like being kind.

> But sometimes I wish I weren't.
> So I can know mercy.

I like being funny.

> But sometimes I wish I weren't.
> So I can know respect.

I like being ambitious.

> But sometimes I wish I weren't.
> So I can know rest.

I like being smart.

But sometimes I wish I weren't.
So I can know peace.

I like being romantic.

But sometimes I wish I weren't.
So I can know love.

I like being me.

But sometimes I wish I weren't.

NO LONGER

You no longer have to worry
about keeping your name out of my mouth.

I'll no longer criticize your relationships,
your ignored privilege, your gifted selfishness.

I'll no longer warn others of your pettiness,
your refusal to forgive, your overreactions.

I'll no longer be unfair in my whining,
calling your flaws to attention without warning.

Your name will no longer leave my lips,
no matter if I'm in the company of enemies or friends.

I'll no longer praise your intellect,
your kind heart, your innate beauty.

I'll no longer think of you first for my news,
my ideas, things you would enjoy.

I'll no longer defend our friendship,

when it clearly no longer exists.

Your name is no longer in my mouth,
as you no longer want it to be.

After the flames burned through everything
And only the ashes remain
Deep in the soot and the black
Is one crisp orange ember
Always burning bright
For a fire that will never die

HALFWAY TO CRAZY

I'm halfway to crazy.
Won't you meet me there?

I travelled all this way
At least meet me halfway

I lost myself and found you
and I don't know what to do

When the map is clear
but I am stuck here

Here in your heart
Worth only what was bought

I'm halfway to crazy
Please meet me.

I fell so deep
That I looked at the devil
And thought of him as an angel

WAKE ME

———————————

Wake me when you are mine.

When the destiny on the road we paved is realized.

When we reach what we've been racing towards at full pace.

When I have you in my arms and can whisper my tenderness to you.

When the stars fit where they are meant to sit.

When my heart belongs to me again.

VENOM

———————————

The last of my humanity has died, replaced by the
venom required to fuel my ambitions.

Have I finally transformed into the monster you
wanted to fear?

Or are you scared that I am now the creature needed
outside of your control?

For my humanity is gone, but the shadow remains.

Darkening your innocence of this death.

GOOD GIRL

———————————————

Such a good girl, they say.
"She calls her parents every day at lunch!"
>   *She's dating a married man because of a hunch.*

Such a good girl.
"I never see her without a smile!"
>   *She was feeling suicidal for a while.*

Such a good girl.
"Not even 25 and published a book!"
>   *What she writes in her diary will leave you shook.*

Stable job, good hobbies, great friends-
>   *Her alcoholism had her on the bends.*

A strong sense of self, loving family -
>   *Please see the real me.*

and she even owns her own home!
>   *She is always alone.*

Such a good girl.
>   *Let me give you a twirl.*

WHAT ARE YOU DOING

————————————————

What are you doing?
Your voice echoes in my ears.
I close my eyes and see nothing but you.
My mind wanders and I think nothing but you.
What are you doing?
Don't you know what is happening to me
How my soul is becoming yours
How my heart belongs to your laugh
What are you doing?
Do you know what you're doing?
Because I'm yours without another word.
What are you doing?

THROUGH THE CURTAIN

Through the curtain I see you

Through the curtain you see me

Together we see the other

But apart the world only sees a curtain
And one lonely soul
Peeking through

BLIND BEGINNINGS

My eye catches no one
but it caught you

Tall, in a room of other strangers
All faces known to me now
But none quite as known as you

If I had known where it would lead
Where we would go
Then maybe I could have looked away

But I didn't
And now I keep looking

Until I am made blind.

SMILE

Put a smile on, girl.
Pretend to be happy.
You have a happy little life.
You have a happy little family.
There's no need to fret.

Put on a smile, girl.
Pretend to be confident.
You have lots of friends.
You have lots of fun.
There's no need to fret.

Put on a smile, girl.
Pretend to be funny.
You have a lot of confidence.
You have a lot of charisma.
There's no need to fret.

Put on a smile, girl.
Pretend to be normal.
You have family.
You have friends.

There's no need to fret.

Put on a smile, girl.
Quit pretending.
Your family has you.
Your friends have you.
You're charismatic.
You're confident.
You're funny.
You have a happy little life.
There's no need to fret.

SACRIFICE

I let the blade sink into my stomach. It was painful. I looked at him, burning the memory of him and his brown eyes into my soul so that it would be the last thing I thought of. That was the folly of love. When even when it pained us, destroyed us, devastated every aspect of our lives, it was still the purest substance we could create between ourselves. It was something worth protecting. I swore to myself that I'd rather die than let my heart be broken by him, let his heart be broken by me. This was me selling my soul to the devil to fulfill that promise.

This was me dying.

MY STARS

———————————

Oh my stars, my stars.
Gift me my love you crafted for me
The one who believes in you too
The one who prays to you and nothing else
Make the pain from his absence be obsolete.
Let our hearts touch the space between you
Oh my stars, my stars
Grant me your divinity through him.

MY SUNSHINE

———————————

You are sunshine.
I am just a ray.

Slow and subtle
You light up my life.

The chime of your voice
The smoothness of your smile

Every night you cradled me to sleep
and every morning you sing me awake.

The sanity to my madness
The caress to my stress.

Comfort when I didn't ask
Love when I didn't know.

To be held in your arms
is to basking in the summer's glow.

I close my eyes and hear your voice

I open my heart and see your smile.

You are sunshine
and I am just a ray.

But together we glow.
Together we dance.

I can't recognize my angels from my demons
They are made of the same blood
They whisper the same songs

A LOVE LETTER TO MY GOLDEN BOY

Before you, I was gray.
A dark blue, cozy in my dismay.

I was unaware of how I felt cold
until I met you and you were gold

A fire in my dark
A song and thought to hark

You bloomed and made me smile
and I begged for it to last a while

My heart sings for you
and all I would do

For your gold is so warm
and your smile is an art form

that I wish to paint and draw
to cause the ice to thaw.

But even the prettiest trees lose their leaves
and I accept the only message I can receive.

Your gold will still always shine
but the truth is that you will never be mine

Please forgive me for if I bask in your glow
to once again prolong my woe

for I am made of gray and cold
and you are made of fire and gold.

Cut me down

String me to a tree

Let the masses see how ugly I can be

Ruin me

Do what you want

Do what you will

Just let me see that smile only meant for me

Just claim me as yours

And I'll take whatever you give me

WAR

I am a soul condemned to be alone in this universe
An acceptance I made peace with
Until you emerged
And waged war against my fate
But you won't claim victory
And the violence left behind
Destroys me more than
If I never found salvation

WHAT THERE WASN'T

I am no longer a dissonant voice among my thoughts

I am real and I am me

Until I sleep.

And forget all that was to happen tonight.

But I wish I wouldn't forget

Being awake and free

Being a character in my own story

Rather than just a dissonant voice in my head

Always observing and never considering

I could join.

ABOUT THE AUTHOR

dora morrigan is an amateur poet.
this is her first published collection of poetry.

contact her at dalygoodbusiness@gmail.com

Visit more books at
dalygoodmedia.com